The Feels

The Moon 🌙

& My Soul

Moonsoulchild

I started writing at 16; I was fascinated with music, the lyrics behind my favorite songs, and the artist that wrote them. I admired how someone could articulate a single feeling. I was captured by how they could make me feel just by listening. Sometimes I found myself in their story; sometimes, I just appreciated the realness of their art. I started writing because I was inspired. I would suppress how I felt. I shrugged it off often. When I discovered how liberating it was to express how I felt, it became my main source of therapy. It wasn't until the end of 2017 I found myself again. I started sharing my work at the beginning of 2018, announcing my first book. I was honored to be a voice for many who couldn't find the words. I was blessed to be accepted for myself so openly. I love being vulnerable. I love being free. I love sharing my story. If you have read my books before, you know I freestyle; I don't have sections or a single format. My writing styles change as you flip the page. My authenticity shows through each page. **I will advise a trigger warning, this is my story**, and I'm reciting it the best way I know how; whether you resonate or not, **I hope you feel me**.

To Me, Ten years ago:

It seemed tensions were high when it came to identifying who you wanted to be. You were confused about where you stood in life and relationships. You held trauma from years of the unknown when it came to a relationship with your father. It was taken from you when he decided the fate for you both. You lived with someone picking up the pieces, but it never changed how you felt. You lived wondering, chasing, and trying hard to suppress those demons. You found temporary pit stops for souls who needed saving and love too. You lived giving your all and loving through every toxic encounter because giving up wasn't in the cards dealt for you.

You knew firsthand what it felt to lose. You began intoxicating yourself, trying to change the reality of everyone around you, so they would grow with you instead of changing your environment. Change never aged well because you feared it. You held on for dear life until you realized not all memories need to hold so much mental space. You didn't know loving someone meant sacrificing yourself in the process. You didn't even realize you attracted yourself to the broken. You convinced yourself the only way you could feel something was to find someone to give that to you. You felt broken, and instead of trying to fix yourself, you tried to love anyone who gave you an ounce of attention. There were many failed attempts at finding someone interested in knowing you. Many sleepless nights were wondering why you weren't good enough. You were wondering how everyone else had it figured out while you were living in the moment, wondering when it would happen for you, to feel something, anything. The problem was you always felt something throughout these moments; you were chasing expectations and nothing that was for you. You wished to be loved when you could have done that all this time. You were right where you needed to be; you just took a lot of detours to get there.

From me, **10 years later**:

    your timing was perfect.

10 years in the future

It makes me uncomfortable to think,
to try and put a timeline on my growth.
To put unsteady expectations
on false hopes.
It makes me uneasy to think
I need to have where I'll be
all planned out.
Why are we taught
that the future is you?
Why not the now, the present?
Why do we feel the need to rush
and chase these fantasies of dreams
we write into our story.
Instead of living, loving
and being present.

The truth is,
I don't know
where I'll be in 10 years,
I didn't know 10 years ago
I'd be here,
but here I am
all because
I didn't fear the outcome.

<u>10 people I needed to let go of:</u>

1. The one who manipulated me, belittled me.

2. The one I outgrew.

3. The one who outgrew me.

4. The one whose memory took up too much mental space.

5. The one good at faking.

6. The pettiness inside me.

7. The shy, timid, and fearful soul inside me.

8. The one who never accepted me.

9. The one who made me feel hard to love.

10. Everyone that couldn't embrace me wholeheartedly.

<u>10 people I'll never forget:</u>

1. The ones who pushed me to my full potential.

2. The ones who inspired me to be the best version of myself.

3. The ones who supported me through my darkest times.

4. The ones who brought light, a different perspective.

5. The ones who kept me grounded, who kept me above the fantasy.

6. The ones who believed in my dreams as much as I did.

7. The ones who accepted me and never disowned me.

8. The ones who didn't treat me like a shy, timid soul, but saw me for who I saw.

9. The ones who loved me through my growth.

10 affirmations when I'm overwhelmed:

1. **I am beautiful.**

2. Everyone's opinions of me don't define me.

3. *I am whole.*

4. The insecurities of others aren't my responsibility.

5. I am more than my flaws.

6. I am an inspiration; I bring light.

7. My past is a reflection of my strength.

8. **I am capable** of everything I deserve.

9. I am *human*; my imperfections aren't mistakes.

10. My mind plays tricks, but it doesn't control me.

Thank you note:

Out of everyone, I'm most grateful for you. I'm blessed to have gotten this far with the capacity of knowledge I hold. I'm blessed to have gone through every situation; even if it brought me a great deal of pain, it also brought me remorse. The pain never changed me; it only brought me a sense of purpose. I chased fantasies more than I chased my dreams. I was confused because I thought they went hand in hand. I was chasing love from people who couldn't give it to me. I was chasing people who weren't meant for me. I lived with trauma from experiences I didn't place myself in, some were out of my control, and some were. I take accountability for the souls I hurt in the crossfire of finding myself. I learned some of the greatest lessons. I'm still opening doors and finding people and things that fit within my journey. I'm still opening old wounds to heal. I'm still trying to love myself in ways I never could. I'm thankful for you, above all, because even after everything you've been through, you're still strong as ever.
I'm so proud of you.

The years with the most impact:
(reflecting)

2007: I was entering high school and starting a new chapter. I didn't know this chapter meant my father disappearing from my life. I was 14 years old; I had no sign of understanding what loss felt like. I didn't know why or how long he'd be gone; at that time, it didn't even feel real. I had a whole family that loved me, but his absence was a void I didn't know I'd blindly try to fill.

2009: a year I'll never forget, the year my family changed. I lost three people in a small amount of time. I was 16; I was in my sophomore year of high school. I didn't have a grip on what it was like to grieve. My Poppy and my cousin Shayla both passed days after each other. My Nana passed in March. They said death always came in three, and I honestly wasn't prepared. I put a lot of the pain on the backburner. I didn't try to understand, I saw everyone in pain, and I didn't want to feel that kind of pain. So the first time I experienced death in front of me, I didn't know what to think, feel, or how to process it.

2012: this is a year I'll never forget because I was over high school, even though it was one of those bittersweet experiences. I despised school until it came to topics I was interested in. I cherished the connections I made the most; those who traveled with me the most. After spending my whole time chasing after a "crush" who played with my emotions and never returned those feelings, I found someone who did. I started talking to them during my junior year, but nothing held it together. We were long-distance; our talks were short and spread out. There was no telling the next time I would fall deeper into this lust. I created more than what was between us. 2012 was the year we finally met in person, and we gave ourselves a shot. It lasted a good four months. It's true; you don't know a person until you open your world to them and see their vulnerable self. His life consisted of parties, friends, and drugs. He became the idea of everything I didn't want in a person. To know I got myself deep into this relationship just to want out. I was blind for so long, but it was also a spiritual awakening. After being blind and vulnerable for so long, I found a piece of myself.

2014: after all the heartache and disappointment, this year, I found love. I saw someone interested in knowing me. It was exciting to find someone and let myself get close to them. When I was over something, there was no going back. I knew what I wanted, and I told myself I would find it. It seems incredible when every situation begins; getting to know someone is an experience I was drawn to. This year brought someone into my life that I didn't think I needed. The beginnings were bittersweet.

2017: if "the worst moment of your life" could be a year, this would be the one. This year was life-changing and transforming. This year brought my purpose and the rest of my life into perspective. On April 17, I lost a soulmate; she was special. It was the moment of my awakening; I never felt the kind of pain I did at that moment ever in my life. I wouldn't wish that kind of pain on my worst enemy. I was 24, compared to when I was 16, and trying to understand death, I could grieve and feel the pain firsthand. Anxiety became my everyday life, and sleep crept up every corner. This is the year I felt so alone, even with people who loved me near. The heartache I felt couldn't be understood, only felt, and I didn't feel like anyone could feel it. Writing found its way back into my life, and I made it through those darkest times. This year I graduated college, lost some of the closest people, and gained new insight into what matters. This year opened my eyes to everything not meant for me. I didn't think it was possible to love so much but feel so much pain at the same time.

2018: the years of pain were behind me. This was the year I became the version of myself I always envisioned. This is the year I became who I loved and was proud of. I released my first book, "The Journey Through My Heart," and created an audience and a vast support system. I was thrilled to be living a dream gifted to me. I kept my talent a secret for so long, but when I finally let myself be free, I found my voice and I found so many who needed to hear what I needed to release. This was the year I walked away from a four-year relationship where I once felt safe. I no longer felt like myself; there wasn't any more growth for us. The lack of communication when it came to the emotions that ran through us. The lack of real support when it came to my passions. It was the actual definition of someone supporting me for their benefit but not in the ways I needed. It was a tough decision to walk away from someone who brought comfort, which ended up being my one problem; I was afraid of change. I never thought it could bring something better for me. When I loved, I gave my all. I couldn't imagine giving love away. I couldn't imagine hurting someone. I was gifted the most valuable lesson this year, that I will make mistakes, and sometimes I needed to create a place of discomfort to grow. Once I opened my eyes to the manipulation and left it all behind, my life started to align with everything meant for me.

I met my best friend this year; I released my first book. He is an author too. I supported his work and opened up to him. There was this undeniable force between us. He understood me in ways no one could; if that wasn't a gift from the universe, I don't know what was. He never threatened my relationship at the time. He listened but always told me to follow my heart. He was authentically himself and helped me open my eyes to everything meant for me. Everything this year happened so quickly. I walked away from someone I was with for years to start a brand-new life. I was afraid. I didn't know what to expect. I didn't think

I'd end up with my best friend the way it happened, some may assume it was planned, but it wasn't. I never planned anything; it was all the universe doing. I lost love; I found love. I found the love that aligned with me. For a year that started with confusion, it ended with so much purpose. I was happy; I was accepted for who I was by someone who saw me for the first time. Everything else is history — everything else after has been wonderful.

2020: incredible blessings that kept going. I quit my 9-5 that I was at for three years and became a full-time author. My book sales were ranking; my platforms were growing. I was able to enjoy life and spend more time where it mattered. My niece was born. Living through a pandemic and so much change in the world, it was a year of so much growth.

Every year after, it's **all blessings** from here.

Self-reflecting:

1. Body image:

Before: I was deeply insecure about my weight growing up; everyone acknowledged me when they saw me for the first time. I never found anything that fit perfectly; I never felt comfortable in anything I wore. People constantly told me I should eat more or asked if I ate enough. I started to visualize myself in the eyes of everyone and believed I wasn't desirable or beautiful because of my size. I was a size 0 until my 20's. I always wondered what it felt like for someone to see me without my physical appearance.

Now: I am no longer that thin girl I was, I've grown, and my body is at a place I adore but always room for growth. I'm happy I am no longer a size 0 because people have placed these stereotypes on me. I have found an eye for myself that no one can take from me. Living in this body, I've learned nothing is constant, not the bad, not the good. I live with bloating and uncertainty when it comes to loving myself. It's a battle I'll always live with, a work in progress.

2. My skin:

Before: Growing up with acne burdened me often. I've been turned down many times due to my skin not being clear. I wasn't desired, and it was out of my control. I felt discomfort. I felt anxiety. I felt ugly. I fell more into my shell when people called out my insecurities and let them define me.

Now: I take pride in the good days when my skin glows. I feel my best when I do my self-care. I love having clean, fresh skin. The summer brings out my best when it comes to the glow. I hate breakouts, and I let myself become defined by them. I let myself be afraid to face them. I needed to accept them.

I remember someone telling me that sharing your insecurities with the public is dangerous, especially on social media, where people can use it against you. I probably would agree if I wasn't aware of my flaws and didn't accept them, but I don't. I feel free when I share my insecurities; it's like they can no longer control me. No one could ever use my flaws against me because I've already lived through the worst of them; hurtful words can't break me anymore.

3. Public speaking:

Before: Social anxiety, in a nutshell, I was mute for most of my childhood. I was nervous when speaking or doing anything in front of a crowd. I couldn't make friends because I didn't trust to let anyone; it was rare. I didn't understand how I felt during these moments, my heart would race, and I would feel light-headed. Sometimes I'd cry. I wasn't easily open; I was reserved. I hated to talk. I hated meeting new people. I hated school projects. I hated reading out loud. I just wish there wasn't so much pressure on getting me to talk. I wish there wasn't so much pressure when acknowledging I was shy. It became my existence, and I prayed for it to fade away.

Now: the anxiety is still a member, but I've opened myself up so much, that being shy is a choice. I'm not huge on surrounding myself with people from my past who were part of the battle of moving past that phase of my life. I'm an introvert and a free spirit; I'm quiet around those I don't know well. One thing that came out of all these years of being shy, I accepted my gift of reading energy before I let it hurt me.

I struggled a lot with my physical image, along with my inner demons. The more I talk about them, the more I heal. My insecurities have lived with me for as long as they've existed. I believe they will always exist; some days are better than others. To fully heal them, I don't think I ever will. There is so much memory I won't ever forget. Each day gets easier to live with my flaws because instead of letting them define me, I let them motivate me to become a better version of myself.

Abandonment Issues

I hated being alone
more than a day,
but I often found myself
hiding away,
because I needed to be alone.
Abandonment issues,
when you feel the need to be close
because everyone you love
seems to drift away
just when you get close.
So,
I would chase
like it was a race
to keep them close.
I thought I needed
their presence to feel safe,
but the chase for their heart
costed me.
Those abandonment issues
were unhealthy attachments
to never face my trauma,
until I came face to face
with my demons.
I was chasing comfort in the people
who left me,
I abandoned myself.

People who live in glass houses

don't see their reflection,
they don't see through their wrongs,
they throw stones
at those who make the same mistakes
they don't see the harm
In hypocrisy.
They see no wrong in their doing
because they don't know what it's like
to take accountability,
they judge
and blame everyone
for the same harm they give.
If only,
living in a glass house meant
being afraid of the damage done
when it all shatters from the outcome,
of the demons that haunt, taunt
and scarred.
Instead,
living in a glass house
meant standing on this pedestal
of narcissistic behavior.

Some people
will never love you
the way you need to be loved,
because they haven't yet
loved themselves in that capacity.

No superpowers

I attracted broken souls so much
I thought it was my calling
to save, fix
and heal them.
I thought if I could,
they would love me.
I caught myself
drowning in their trauma,
I ended up almost broken
trying to mend them together.

Hallucinations

If I love you,
I love you until I'm incapable.
When the times get dark.
When the relations become unhealthy.
When the love turns to codependency.
When I finally open my eyes
to whom you truly are,
not who you manipulated me
to believe you were.

The worst feeling I ever felt,
was not being deserving of love
because you made me believe it.
The way you manipulated me,
the way you made me believe
you needed it more than me.

- *why couldn't we both be worthy?*

The fantasy

I never said "I love you"
and didn't mean it,
but I sure did stay long after,
I didn't feel it.
It was hard to grasp
our forever didn't exist.

Darkest Hour

I know I hurt you in the crossfire to save myself. I acknowledge that pain. I loved you through your darkest hour; you brought me to mine. Have you admitted why you couldn't save me, and I needed to save myself? The reckoning that became of us only hurt more, holding on. The pain we endured being entangled together made us feel like we needed each other. So, It hurt like hell for you when you realized I didn't need you. That your manipulative ways couldn't trap me. That your call for help didn't awake my savior complex. I'm done trying to save you when you didn't care to be; you only cared about ruining me.

Talking to myself

I refuse to stay in an environment I outgrew and in those selfish ways. I refuse to keep remembering the good times and convince myself I will feel them again, from the same situation I outgrew that left me with a great deal of pain. I refuse to believe this was all for nothing, so I chose to take a step back and see the beauty in it. I decided to choose growth. I decided to leave behind what no longer served me. The love I felt was real. The love I received was as honest as I thought. The past was now a figment of my imagination; it no longer mattered when it came to everything I was about to endure. I wasn't soaking in the pain of before. I wasn't counting the scars. My heart couldn't take the constant reminding of the pain, so I set myself free of it. I once chose to stand still and fight for a broken love without the skills to repair it. It was the way I loved the broken, the way I couldn't love myself; that's the reason I gave it to everyone else. Someone deserved that love; I didn't think I did. Once I saw the light, I didn't look back. I chose to enjoy the journey, not to let it burden me.

Coming out

I don't think there was a time I stopped time to announce I intimately loved women. I didn't keep it a secret, nor did I scream it from the rooftops. I loved who I loved, and the ones who couldn't accept it, tried to justify it; it's probably a "phase." But, the ones who love me never changed their perception of me. Why would it? It shouldn't be a secret, but we live in a world coming out is the scariest time because we're made to believe love doesn't conquer when it comes to the same gender. You're manipulated to think; you're a disgrace, and that you don't deserve the same blessings because your "**love is love**" Isn't love at all. So, we hide and throw away the key to the deepest secrets we're forced to keep because being free and open could mean a death sentence. The words overplayed still hurt, their unresolved trauma and hate within their heart they can't undo, so they must choose you to break down, to mold, and for you to hide into someone you're not. So, I said, fuck "coming out" I don't owe anyone an explanation, especially when it comes to love.

There's no point
In reviving old connections,
they will never be or feel the same.

Connections

Aren't always meant to be more.
Some are only meant to be felt.
Some are meant to be platonic.
Some aren't meant for you at all.

Second chances

are worth giving,
but don't let yourself drown
In too many second chances.

Stranded heart

We were both
searching for help
to repair our hearts.
I fixed them,
as they almost broke me.
That's why the ending was fast,
because I exploded
with rage, I had caged in,
I broke free.

Ghosting 101

If I ever walked away,
It was calculated,
and I felt it was best for me.
I would never walk away
and hurt someone intentionally.
I would never hurt someone I love
for my gain.
I never walk away
until presented with no other option,
that's when I choose myself.

I could read energy so well
until it came to someone
who lied about their intentions,
someone who faked their love for me.
Or perhaps I did know,
I just bet my heart
they'd end up loving me.

-     *It left me in debt*

A dose of manipulation

I was lost. I used my love as a weapon and sometimes a manipulation to be loved in return. I wanted to feel loved. I wanted to feel how good it felt to be in love. I tried to create it within a lot of the wrong ones. I tried to save and fix everyone while damaging myself. I couldn't recognize the real from the phony because I let myself be vulnerable and blinded by my need to be loved. I set up my heartbreak. I couldn't trust anyone; I let them get close only to push them away.

My darkest hour
was also my biggest wake-up call.
I opened my eyes,
I decided to heal from it all.

Growth

will sneak up on you
In many ways,
It will free you
but hurt you too.

We all give love a bad name
when it comes to the heartache
of trying to make someone
love us the same.

I haven't spoken to everyone from **my past** and apologized for the pain I caused them. I hope they don't feel the weight of my mistakes surrounding their heart. Who I was then is far from who I am now. I was lost then, but I found myself.

I always pray for them.

I hope they realize who they are is someone worthy of love. I hope they love themselves with that same love too. I hope they made peace with the demons of their trauma and learned to overcome those dark times, and accepted the pain they brought too.

The past

Being lost, I can relate to bringing unwanted pain from pettiness without thinking clearly. I didn't know who I was; I didn't know who was there for me. I felt as if it was me, and everyone was against me. So, I apologize for only blaming you. I apologize for the pain I caused for ghosting you. You didn't deserve to wonder. You didn't deserve to be left with this result of me that wasn't the finished product. I was petty; that's not who I wanted you to love.

If you had the chance to know who I am now, I believe you would love me. I think you would be proud of me. I think our friendship would be embraced without feeling the need to control every outcome. We would be free within each other and the beauty that comes with it. We were alike; that's where we collided. We could have used that to conquer and become stronger; instead, it became a constant competition, and our love became tainted.

I believe our love would conquer because we have grown and the love we always had for another was hidden away and afraid to show because of our insecurities; we placed them onto each other and let them become us.

I believe in second chances in certain situations when two people both did wrong and not intentionally, two lost souls searching. I believe there may be a chance for us again, in this life, or maybe we don't get one at all. Even if we never speak again, I think of you often. I pray for you. I never held any grudges toward you because you were my best friend. My identity and direction in life were in question. I let that interfere with our friendship.

I'm sorry for hurting you in the crossfire.

<u>A message to a platonic soulmate:</u>

I know I'm probably the last person you wish to hear from, but honestly, it took me a while to reach out after all these years. I had dreams. I think about you often. I know everything that went down with us was long ago, and bringing that up again may not be necessary, but I wanted to apologize for the hurt I brought you. Back then, I didn't know the life I was living, nor was I sure of who I wanted to be. 2018 was a year of change and so much realization, and everything came into perspective for me. I thought about reaching out sooner, but I thought I'd be a fool after never texting you back, but at the time, I didn't know how to handle it, and I thought us being apart would help the on-and-off thing we had. I feel we were both misunderstood by our feelings, and I let people dictate those feelings. You were my best friend, and I let that go, and I don't expect you ever to understand my reasoning or ever to respond. So I'm not writing this to hear forgiveness.

I'm writing this to free myself from feeling like I could have done something different. I know what I did was wrong; I could have talked it through, but I thought what I was doing was right at the moment, so I stood by it. After years went by, I felt maybe we could talk it out, and perhaps we'd find ourselves in a place where we are completely whole and sit and talk, more importantly, understand both views and see we both brought each other heartache. I can't discredit how I made you feel because they're your feelings. I just want you to know; that I was blinded by a life that wasn't for me, and I should have listened to you. My free spirit self got lost, especially when I felt like I lost everything, including myself. I was always proud of you. I was always rooting for you. I was always there when you needed to share your wins and when you needed to cry. I'm sorry if I made you feel like you couldn't come to me or if I made you feel like I was against you. I was always on your side.

We were so much alike in ways it made us collide. Remember the days when we were younger and when we would share our writing? When were we carefree in ways the world didn't let us be pinned against each other? I know those days are gone, but sometimes I feel we didn't fight hard enough against everything trying to break us. I should have listened to my intuition and should have listened to you when it came to certain people and things that weren't right for me. Maybe it wasn't our time. Maybe our time was cut short. I don't know, but I'm grateful for every great memory we shared. I want you to know you brought tremendous value to my life even after we parted. I may have written pieces with pettiness, but I was hurt and confused; that's a part of how I felt, and I can't undo the damage done. I've grown these past four years, and I learned so much about myself and about connections and how important it is to express how I feel even if it doesn't benefit me in the way I want it to. I know this message isn't what you're expecting. I honestly don't know what to expect or if you missed me all these years or if you hate me. I deserve to wonder after ghosting you. I don't expect a response. I just needed to free myself from this pain my heart was left for by my mistakes. I hope you're happy, loved, and getting everything you deserve. I always pray for you. I'll always love you.

A best friend heartbreak
Is the hardest heartbreak of all.

Games I lost

Some people didn't deserve
the capacity of love I gave.
They took advantage of
every bit of good in me.
They knew I'd forgive them
so, they played me.
I ended up breaking myself
trying to make them love me.

Puzzles

As I tried to mend everyone I loved
and save them
from everything hurting them,
I blindsided myself,
I didn't see myself crumbling
Into the same pieces
I was trying to pick up for them.

The most challenging relationship
Is discovering yourself
After the one
that made you lose yourself,
the toxic one.

Your unresolved trauma
will end up hurting everyone,
including you
in the crossfire.
When you try and love them
with a broken heart.

I wasn't healed,
I was damaged
trying to love another
without being over the last,
wishing to have that old thing back.

-    *not over you*

A love story that ended badly

It was a game
I played fairly
but got cheated terribly.
I convinced myself
I was broken,
that without you,
I'd never breathe again
until I suffocated in your presence.
letting you go
was my biggest win,
and *that would be an understatement.*

Hostage

You never deserved me
In any way
shape
or form,
you never deserved to know me
from the depths of my soul
to every beat of my heart,
but I let you,
I let you.
For far too long
I replayed this song
hoping the lyrics changed,
that our story could somehow transform
so, I'm no longer trapped
In the force of your possession
and I could somehow
break out of your prison.

To heal is to hurt
but to know,
the outcome will bring you through.

Protect your heart.
Protect your soul.
Protect that beautiful
aura of yours
from this **cold world***.*

*Not everyone deserves
your unconditional love.
Sometimes your love needs
to be conditional,
under the terms
of being reciprocated.*

I realized it was wrong to be upset when someone vocalized how I made them feel, even if I didn't share the same view. I can't justify someone's feelings; they felt that way for a reason. I had to accept it and hope never to make someone feel that way again.

Heartbreak PTSD

I couldn't love you
the way you needed me to,
so, I couldn't keep you close.
Having you near was only destroying me,
the damage I was left with for years.

I wasn't a savior,
I attracted the broken
because I knew firsthand how it felt
to feel your lowest.
I thought if I could save them,
love them,
and help them see their worth
I wouldn't need to pick up my pieces.
I was a broken soul
searching for the same I was giving.

I pushed people away
so, they couldn't hurt me.
I pushed people away
and expected them to fight for me.
I tried to prove my love
by saving and fixing
every broken soul
so that they would love me.
I was blaming love
when it was me,

- *I was chasing everything but peace.*

I'm terrible at letting go
because of the nostalgia of
"what used to be"
and how good it once felt.
I'm awful at painting a new picture
of whom they grew to be.
I'm terrible at change,
It was,
"if I love you, I'll love you forever."
It broke me
realizing it was just a fantasy.

Maybe you never deserved to love me
because of the many times you hurt me.
Perhaps I never deserved to love you.
Maybe you didn't deserve someone who
kept the story going until it became toxic.

Gravity

I was soul-searching when I found you.
Your heart's language was like a vacation to
my soul. Your tenderness was a breath of
fresh air. You craved me in ways I always
praised. Every part of me I tamed and held
hostage, I set free. You never shamed me for
not being whole, but you didn't feel the
need to save me. The force that led me to
you, I never questioned it; it's the closest to
the moon I've ever been. You're the
reflection of all the good I am. It's when I
stopped trying to force my story, I
discovered you. You are the definition of
my soul's twin.

It's **magic**,
being tangled with you
I never felt love so free,
so superhuman
because it's you,
It will always be you.

Morning After by DVSN

It was the soundtrack of our love,
that whole weekend we made love
to every song,
but morning after
brought the greatest climax.
Something about you,
the anticipation of you,
the lyrics spoke the words
I couldn't tell,
so, I let them tell
as I showed you.
My mind was cluttered with confusion
but my body made up for it.
I never wanted someone so much
my body felt the rush,
It's never been to that special place
but you took me there,
not once,
every single time in every song.
that night was special,
I discovered DVSN
while I devoured in you.
I knew at that moment
I wanted to make love to you
and only you,

until the end of our time,
until sunrise,
like we did that whole weekend
like it was the last time.
My body trusted you
and my heart loved you,
you were my escape,
my safe place.

I'll never forget the first time we made love
and the orgasm my soul felt
knowing it was you,
the one who made my body smile.

A piece of jewelry with meaning

No piece of jewelry ever impacted me, nor was it ever real, until you gifted me something more than a material item. It was a moment of bliss, undeniably unforgettable, the look on my face when you presented our forever within this moon stone ring. Something you took the time to choose. Something that held so much meaning. It didn't matter the size. It didn't matter the way you presented it. At that moment, I felt our forever when I knew you picked it with me in mind; you took the time to remember the things I adored and imprinted them into our forever. You knew no material thing could ever amount to the love I have for you, but that didn't stop you from finding the perfect ring. My passion for the moon and my love for you are imprinted together.

Love note

Our journey was the one that put everything in my life into perspective. I watched myself fall apart in front of you as you caught me every time. A friend you were, my first author friend. I trusted you, a connection of a force that brought us closer. Facetime calls. Poems. Secrets unleashed; you knew it all so early on. I opened my heart to you; I wanted you to know me, the real me, not the person I've been pretending to be out of fear. You knew my imperfections, the secrets of my many mistakes. I knew if this was going to be anything, I needed to be honest.
My chance to start over and not dim me, to be who I knew myself to be all along. The part that got me was when you accepted all of me. It's like being honest drew us closer together, and that's not something I was used to. The way you made me feel was different; being someone who felt like I was never understood or completely loved for everything I am, I found everything in you. I was terrified to leave everything I once knew, everything that brought me comfort.

I was afraid to see you and had no idea what we would become; knowing we lived 1,200 miles apart, how could we make this work? I constantly tried to find the proper storyline. I was confused, but the universe came and made it make sense when you moved here with me, and we made a home within each other. We're engaged. It's been three years growing with you. Our time is always cherished. The time, support, and love we fill each other with is a blessing. I will always be your best friend and supporter. I will stand by you until the end of time. I don't ever question it because I know you will always reciprocate back. To the moon and never come back. Our love is timeless. *Thank you* for always being the man I love and can count on. You are everything and more.

I *genuinely* fell for someone I didn't see coming. I was on the road to self-discovery when I found my best friend. I wasn't searching to be loved; I was growing and finding my peace. It's like my prayers were finally answered; my sanctuary was complete.

Something about you
brings déjà vu.
Our love and you
have felt so familiar,

- *my past life lover*

A soulmate

I fell in love with souls, many
not even romantically
an undeniable connection
embedded in the stars,
we aligned
a friendship created from the scars,
our secrets unleashed,
the freedom of comfort
in the darkest times turned to light,
like the moon at night
they all brought beauty to my life,
even if it was just a spark
or a flame,
our fate was written.
I'm so happy we collided
even if our story can't be forgiven.

Wasted times

Many fleeting moments I chased,
hoping they would be something.
The time wasted,
chasing a moment that was broken.
I was soft,
my tender heart fell for anyone
who made it feel something.

Mirror talks

I don't understand why they couldn't see you. I don't know why they couldn't feel the vibrations your soul radiates; instead, they rather sympathize with your flaws and dilute them until you're begging to be set free of your insecurities. I don't understand why they couldn't love you past your physical curse. I don't know why you couldn't be desired because something jeopardized their taste.

But you, you always saw them. You always felt every fleeting moment. You always questioned their intentions. You always caught every sign. You also felt every stimulating moment. You weren't biased; you even loved those who were broken. You were often seen guilty for trying to mend them, failing every time, you weren't their savior, but they were your kryptonite.

They never deserved to feel you; that's why they couldn't ever see you.

Transparency

I sometimes treat the people I loved
like a temporary void,
a fleeting moment.
I never trusted the euphoric vibrations,
I treated them like broken promises.
My vice was the chase,
the desire of being craved,
I wanted to feel wanted.
I couldn't trust anyone to love me
If I searched for voids to fill me.
If I couldn't vow
to give that same love to myself.

Self-accountability

I volunteered as tribute
for the wreckage of my life
I made a mess of.
To the broken, the fragile, and the hurting:

1. I should have loved you with more empathy and less shame.

2. I should have watered your roots with reassurance and less tragedy.

3. I should have kept you safe with consistency and less nostalgia.

4. I should have had the courage to heal you without hurting you.

5. I should have told you your home will never be found in anyone but you; maybe you wouldn't be a home to vacant souls.

6. I should have saved you, but without the aching pain that touched you, you wouldn't see the magic in you, let alone believe it to be true.

My condolences

To anyone who lost me, to anyone I set free. I was tired of shrinking myself to your conflicted and confusing possession of who you wanted me to be. I was exhausted trying to worship something I envisioned, something that never bloomed. I was depleted trying to feel your hues, but all I felt were the blues. My condolences to you for never seeing me for the majestic view I was; you just saw the reflection of you.

In this maze with you,
one you placed me in
and never told me the rules.
Depleted,
I went in circles
searching for you.

Loving you with my whole heart
but also letting you know
when you're wrong,
a **love language**.

Connections & Security

I never had sex with anyone I didn't have a connection with, even if it wasn't love, even if it never became a relationship, there was a connection. If it was small, if it ended up just being a friend, I still felt comfort and a deeper force. To give myself to anyone on a soul level was rare. I'm introverted but have a free spirit. What you got from the outside looking in didn't even begin to scratch the surface. Being someone who felt uncomfortable my first time, something traumatic I forever have embedded in my mind; I need that source of comfort to even get close to anyone.

Being free made some believe otherwise because of how open I chose to be. I have no shame in who I am; I have found peace in my love for myself. I love sharing that love with the world.

You read about it when it comes to my soul, but not everyone feels it. Even after breaking down those walls, I built to protect my heart, I always kept a guard. The ones who've been close to me made me feel something, a connection deep enough to make me feel alive and comfortable at the same time. When it came to love, I seemingly became a fool every time I let anyone in, but it was rare when my heart and soul matched. It was the purest and most peaceful love I ever felt when it finally did. I will continue to soak in that love for as long as I have it.

Imperfectionist

It's not about finding the perfect person; it's about finding the person who fits perfectly with you. The person who has dreamt the same vision. The person who shares the same passionate ambition. The person who creates light from their darkness. The person who holds the same strength when the universe isn't always aligned with them. The perfect person doesn't exist in the form of perfection you know to be. The ideal person is the one who challenges you, who makes you take a step back and see you from their perspective, the one who brings a different narrative than the one you're used to. The perfect person will inspire you to be your best self by helping you test your limits by breaking the fear that built them. The perfect person will not come easy, nor will they be difficult. The perfect person will be soft; they will love you in a way you've never been touched, a soul experience; they dig deep into the part you're afraid to go. They will guide you to your healing, the wrenching pain that's beneath the surface. It's a beautiful disaster to find out some will stay around, and some will stay as long as they're written. It's essential to know the perfect person doesn't exist. We're all searching and chasing to find ourselves. We're all damaged souls searching for acceptance, love, and a feeling we've yet to experience. Things to remember, love is always beautiful. Cherish every moment, and nothing is permanent.

Everyone's expectations of me aren't my responsibility. I don't need to fit this standard of what you made of me. I'm not the mirror of your insecurities; you don't get to nitpick me. If you aren't going to love me for who I am, let me go, don't continue to use me.

Self-destruction

I had my heart broken
the same way I broke hearts.
I manipulated myself
the same way I let myself be used.
I sat and waited
for the universe to align me
perfectly with the one.
I passed up some
for the wrong ones
I wrecked some
for the broken ones
I wanted to prove my love,
I wanted to be loved
truly, madly, deeply
I couldn't grasp
I was the broken one
and my path of destruction
brought me closer
to the shattered ones.

To the men who broke my heart:

I'm thankful it was only a fracture, even though it felt like an eternity to heal. I carried the bruises with me like a warrior; I had to; my picture of love then was a battlefield. Your inconsistency was humiliating, but I kept clinging and hoping for reassurance. I'm very selective now; back then, I voluntarily chose pain if there was a chance it was linked to love. I let go of my morals when I became fluent in choosing empty promises. I hoarded the beautiful moments. My vision became blurry when my heart's language wasn't matched. My soft heart didn't deserve to be stained with your cheap version of love. I craved a connection so tender that you seemed to taint with your chaotic ways. Your conviction still haunts me, but the lessons are embedded deep inside me and attainable when I need them to resurface, to remind myself to never settle for the echoes of your cheap potential ever again.

To the woman I loved:

I wasn't ready for your love, I admit it. I was timid at the thought of letting myself close. I didn't know what it would be like to open myself to you. I built this wall that turned into a whole space; I trapped myself deep inside it. Your essence was mesmerizing; I felt it as soon as we locked eyes. Your aura was as comforting as the waves hitting the ocean under the moon. Your soul was wild but tamed when your soft heart came into play. Being free was the melody you set in your harmonic ways. I adored you. I became fearless after losing you; I couldn't take the chance of being afraid to ever let someone love me as I did you. The rush I still get from thinking of you, the canvas I painted of you, the smile that captivated me way back then, it's all faded into this forsaken place in my soul. I need you to know; that I will love you endlessly; I just placed you there alone. You're a void I don't ever want to fill.

The attachment I placed on everyone
Just to find love,
One I never got to feel
Because they all disappeared
Like the stars at night
When the clouds wanted their time to shine.
My heart was a storm,
A tornado of uncertainty,
When it came to love
I whispered, "help me find the one."
Every night, endlessly
Until I suffocated from the pain.
My heart was starving,
Shattered
And drowning
Because of my symphony
With the blues,
My "I love you"
Seemed to be cursed
Because every "I love you too"
was nonexistent
or a daydream
I kept reminiscing.

Unrequited Love

A different kind of heartache comes with a love that isn't returned. There's a different story in both views, one is blinded while the other is leading. It's like a trip down love lane, but you end up down the road of disappointment. You become misled by the love you feel; you convince yourself their intentions match yours with an ounce of what feels like love. It's like losing someone you never had, something that can't be explained because it never made sense. After all this time, you tried hard to make it feel right, and the universe always presented the signs it was never for you. It feels like getting your heart ripped out of your chest and never getting it back. It feels like all the past love you felt wasn't real. You start to question your intentions and heart. We place so much power on what we did wrong without holding them accountable for leading us to believe there was something more. We blame ourselves for falling. We blame ourselves for love. We blame ourselves for being blind to what we thought we felt. It's not our heart's fault we felt something for them; changing the way we love should never be discussed. Why do we always need to change when we become hurt? Like loving and being honest is wrong. Sadly, we convince ourselves to be heartless and cold when we become heartbroken. We become afraid to open ourselves to someone else because we're scared they'll hurt us too. I can't believe I ever questioned my worth, intentions, and heart for someone who couldn't be honest about theirs. I never deserved to be treated like my heart wasn't enough just because they weren't the one.

Seventeen

How bittersweet a number could feel, your
last breath and your new life meet.
Heartache and a rush of passion, I feel
every year, on April 17,
I fear the thought of you when you
approach, but something about the power
of you near, the strongest ever
I love the tears
I love looking to see the moon full
Because I know,
You're here.

Ten

It seemed my life aligned in every magical
moment when ten was involved.

July **10**, *2018*
We made our love official.

August **10**, *2018*
We started a life together.

November **10**, *2018*
We created a home within each other.

10 years ago, I was searching for the love
that matched mine. **10** years later,
The universe aligned me with you.
I don't find this a surprise; we were always
embedded together. Nothing this powerful
could be forced. If I knew ten was the
number, I would have waited ten more for
you.

Your comfort zone
will only suffocate you deeper
into staying in an environment
you want to grow from.

Teachers who inspired me

This is a letter to all the teachers I admire.
The ones who believed in me and never
gave up on me when I didn't take my
dreams seriously. There were moments
when I needed an extra push; sometimes, I
could not understand because my
comprehension wasn't at the same level as
everyone around me. I was shy, lost, and
full of anxiety. I couldn't force myself when
it came to something I wasn't interested in. I
despised math. I was not too fond of
anything that couldn't capture my attention.
I needed something stimulating, something
I'd seek to know more of. My attention span
wasn't there, and many teachers made it
hard to focus; they were there to collect a
check and do their job; I don't blame them.
But, I grew many connections within the
group of people in the environment I was
placed in. I met some of the most incredible
friends I'll always cherish. I met some of the
greatest teachers, who were there not only
for my needs but believed I would achieve
everything I wanted without the barrier
placed upon me. Their inspiring ways

helped guide me. Their talks helped me light the way to feel safe where I was and where I was headed. I was taught so much but not the books I read or the formula I was trying to break when I think of school. It taught me I had something special within me, and it made me bold. I may not have been book smart, but I was brilliant when it came to life and the whole aspect of what I wanted from it. I'm grateful I had incredible influences who showed me I could live a dream. Sometimes I struggle with understanding the first time around, but I struggle with a bunch; I wasn't going to let it define me.

To the teachers I cherished,
You taught me so much more than any book could.

BOW WOW

I was twelve when I discovered you,
Everything about you, I adored
From your music
To your movies,
I stan.
I supported every venture
I stood with you through it all
I swore I was your number-one fan
Here I am, sixteen years later,
I'm twenty-eight and in line to meet you
I'm frozen
while listening to the voices around me
they all love you,
but in my heart, I'll always love you more.
Frozen without words, I hug you
It's like my childhood flashes before me
A humble man,
Kindhearted
And grateful.
I'm so happy I chose you,
Someone who never disappointed me,

Someone who was unapologetically them.
A legend of my generation,
a man of passion
a performer I'd pay to see every time.
The way your energy lit the room,
we felt it,
your love for your craft,
your love for us.

An idol,
an inspiration.

I'm so proud to say it's you,
thank you for confirming
there was always a reason I loved you.

Knowing I found my person, sometimes I dwell in the moment and smile. Sometimes I soak in the happiness and am blessed to have found a beautiful, healthy, and at-home kind of love. To have found growth and inspiration. You are my favorite soul experience.

Heal yourself
before you let anyone too close,

-    *save them the emotional abuse*

Find someone
who brings the softest love,
who feels like home.
But also, someone
who exposes your truths,
who bares your soul.

Savior complex

A cry for help
I will never turn away,
my heart is too soft
to ever turn a blind eye
to the hurting.

I wanted to feel the softest parts of you,
to unleash those naked truths.
I wanted to pick up the pieces
to justify somehow why they left you.
I didn't want you mourning,
slowly drifting away from reality.
I didn't want you to harden, become cold,
and think what you had was a mirage.
Except it was,
It wasn't love.

-    *I betrayed you making you believe it was*

If I could retrace our love
And take back the compromises I made
To be in sync with you
I would, in a heartbeat.

You poisoned me,
I rejected every antidote
You injected into me
Gaslighting and manipulation
Your spell of choice.

This time,
I'll cast the spell,

-   *No more conditional traits*

I was a revolving door to fleeting moments.
I justified my insecurities often. The
wounds are impacted and unfinished.
Every time that fleeting moment crawled
back, I dealt with the consequences and
reminded myself the mirror was a mirage. I
convinced myself it was me who deserved
to be punished, so I picked apart myself one
more time. I found something new I didn't
like every time someone left me. I didn't
believe in my softness. I didn't think I could
be breathtaking because someone always
managed to crush that reflection. I don't
know why I let them hold my power, to
give them the slightest investment on my
soul. Being desired was always fleeting; I
needed to be empowered.

We meet such great people throughout our lives. Ones that help us grow, inspire us and love us. It's a beautiful and magical thing. It hurts like hell when they leave this world, and all you have left is the memory; that's real heartbreak.

You can't break someone who found themselves after being lost for so long. The broken wall was rebuilt, this time with strength and self-worth. Your insecurities aren't mine; I won't confuse that. I refuse to let someone who's broken try to break me.

Some people will always hold a special place in your heart; you will always love them; they teach you so much. They don't always stay, but you will never forget the time you got with them.

-     *a soulmate*

I detached myself
from everything temporary.

-   *It was hard to believe in your magic.*

There was no question
whether they would still love me
if I didn't love myself,

- *how else would they critique me?*

Loving an artist

There's this captivating story of loving an artist — a story that can be chaotic, but under the impression, you don't understand. There's a certain emotional depth that comes with loving an artist. When you're unaware, their passion seems like loose ends. You may find it daunting how overprotective they can be when it comes to something they love. You may think it's miraculous how they can put emotions into words to make something so beautiful and vivid, something you can relate to. The part of the story you won't ever understand, they're not just pouring their heart out for you. They're opening wounds decades-old to free themselves of the demons they let shadow them. They volunteer to share these therapy sessions but don't expect to be criticized for feeling and being human. The way the mind of an artist is puzzled, it's a wanderer. The way the heart is carved, it's delicate. The way the soul of an artist is exposed, the melody isn't one often remembered. Artists are incredibly misunderstood, but when an artist loves you, you will never die.

Start putting passion
into what fills your soul.
Start putting passion
into your art.
Nothing fleeting,
not people.

- *What's your magic when no one's
around?*

I expected you to lust for me
That entanglement with temptation,
I yearned for it.

-    *Why didn't you crave me?*

<u>Compliments</u>

It was never easy for me to accept compliments. I never knew if it was genuine. I had many "friends" whose agenda wasn't what they presented. They would hold my comfort close and trash me behind my back when it came to their friend who was the bully. It was hard to tell a compliment from a judgment or even a joke. So, it was hard to accept I was beautiful because I'd been lied to; too many times, I confused it, brushed it off, and laughed. It became my defense mechanism. Compliments weren't ever to be trusted.

Personal beliefs

I don't speak on my beliefs out loud; I don't
always feel it's needed or anyone's
business. What you do with your life is
your personal belief to choose what you
think is suitable for your being. No one has
the right to tell you what to do, with your
body, or your voice, or decide what's right
for you. It's you, only you; no one has the
right to make you feel small because of your
decisions. No one has the right to
manipulate you into believing you're a
terrible human for being you. It's not their
choice; it's yours.

Hello,

I'm not writing you this because I think you
deserve forgiveness. I'm not here to give
that to you. All these years, I'm sure you're
wondering if I ever forgave you. You tried
to come back a dozen times to show your
remorse, but you never got close. Isn't it
something you once had my heart in your
hands to destroy within minutes? If the
question is why I never forgave you, it's
because I didn't need to heal and move
forward. I took those pieces you destroyed,
and I threw them out and decided to love
myself instead. I chose to start fresh. I took
the experience of being manipulated and
gaslighted to see through you.
When it was time to leave you, I had no
remorse. I didn't feel bad for leveling up
and doing how you deserved; even then, I
don't think you cared. I never broke you. I
never touched those parts of your soul as

you did mine. You had my heart and soul in this box and kept them closed while you held me close. You played on my love for you; you knew I'd do anything, so you kept playing me. You bet on my love every time, and it cost me. The pain never touched you. I fell into this illusion of love, this dream of what we could be. I chased for you to love me for so long that I became blinded by my own heart. The time you took advantage of me, the times I said no. When it came to your vices, you did "for a good time" but ended up in an entirely different mind space when coming down. I was there for you after all the attempts at breaking me. I know that's my fault, but who I fell for wasn't that person; it was someone who didn't exist. I guess I was hoping you would come through and everything you once promised would come true.
Instead, I have memories of a trauma-filled first time, sexually, emotionally, and mentally. My body, heart, and soul have been scarred from the pain you left behind. The pain will forever live within my heart, but it hasn't taken over my life; I made peace with it. You gave me a story I can tell forever; I wouldn't be proud of that. I don't think you deserve forgiveness because you

chose everything over me. I don't think you deserve forgiveness because none of this would have happened if you didn't intentionally hurt me. I forgave myself for dealing with someone like you; that's enough for me. I built myself back up differently. I'm healed, and you won't get access to who I am now. Why do you think you deserve my forgiveness when you can't admit to a thing you did, to almost shatter me?

The amount of weight someone shows
when it comes to their trauma,
is nothing compared
to the weight they feel.

- *it's called fake smiles for a reason*

Even a *fleeting moment*
can be **beautiful**

Everything I chased
wasn't for me,
but I sure worked overtime
trying to make it be.

The EX I wouldn't date again

I don't know what I saw in you; looking at you now, the thought entirely sickens me. You would think after all these years, I'd be able to forgive you. I guess I do hold grudges, a least when it comes to you. I could never forgive someone who toyed with my heart just to break it. Who built this anticipation of being with, from words with empty meaning. I don't know what it was about you, maybe since you shared the same passion for writing. Your way with words had me high, too high I overlooked those red flags and the undeniably awful thing in front of me. You swore you loved me, but the constant race for your love had me weak. It was me, but it was her too. The late nights I was waiting for you to come home from after-parties, high off molly because that was the cool thing to do. I will never forget you for trying to intoxicate me with your drug of choice. Also, your illusion of love, that toxic love you injected into my vulnerable soul. It's true; some soulmates aren't meant for forever. Some are a lesson. I learned mine with you. There's nothing in life I regret, except for you.

I don't deserve
to be loved in half.
I deserve
to be yearned
for my **wholeness**.

If you push me away,
there's no guarantee
I'll forgive you, let alone forget you.
This obsession
with me being your possession,
don't get it twisted,

-   *it was always a privilege.*

Talking to myself

I feel the most secure when I reassure myself; that I will always conquer. People always make talking to yourself seem weird or make you insane, but I call it therapy. I need to be the one telling myself it will be okay. I need constant reassurance, and it can't come from anyone but myself. I know the fear I'm drowning in and the emotions I dwell in; no one can pinpoint how I feel. I'm the one who decides when to go. I'm the one who picks up the pieces. I'm the one who holds on because I'm too forgiving. I'm the one who battles my own identity, so who else is to save me than me? I think about it often. I ponder it. I wonder where I would be without those 2 A.M. therapy sessions with my notebook. I wonder how healed I would be if I had let everyone decide for me. I always chose a different path, an intuitive one. I always preferred to be my leader. Days where anxiety wins. Nights when my mind goes to that dark hour. I will always conquer. I won't let fear create a monster out of me.

Peaceful:

I am secure. I am soft. I only want radiant energy surrounding me. I don't have questionable love in me. I don't feel the need to prove or chase a void. It was the first time I felt the weight lifted. I feel free. I finally feel the manifestation I put into each mantra I wrote. I finally believe it.

Celebrated:

One thing I loved more than anyone was my passion. My talents. It was one compromise I wasn't willing to make. I would rather lose you if you didn't believe in me. I was always proud of the small wins. I was proud regardless. I recognize my success. I gave myself the flowers everyone gave everyone else. I won't ever wait until I die to be a miracle. To conquer everything against me, I had to let go of the weight of the fear I had against me.

Bold:

I vow never to sugarcoat my truth. Always be brutally honest. To always be free, to never tame my beautiful.

I realized,
communication didn't matter
If you couldn't comprehend.
The slightest misunderstanding
could be an impulse to abandon
and ghost.

-    *Silence seemed like the high road*

Talking to myself II

I woke up one morning and decided to trust my manifestations. I trusted the process. I spoke to myself often. I had many talks with my inner layer. I made my entire environment uncomfortable until I unpacked the trauma. I spent nights sleeping next to a stranger, one I loved because of my heroic behavior. I had a thing for the cold-hearted, thought my softness could somehow warm them. I thought I could stop them from being a fugitive to their own heart. I spoke mantras until I felt the vibrations. Withdrawing from old patterns. Shedding old layers. Unlocking new doors. Building new bridges. I crossed new paths. I found myself in different souls, from different views. I appreciated myself in ways I never was able to. I don't believe in perfection, so you'll always catch me soul-searching; this isn't my final destination, but I sure do enjoy the vacations.

Healing can get dark,
but there's so much beauty
in the darkness

- *I said to the moon*

Talking to myself III

I'm not sure why I wanted to safe keep every soul in distress. I'm not entirely convinced it was because I made myself accessible to them. I do have theories. I think the need to sympathize wasn't enough, so I overprioritized them. I pled guilty to a crime I didn't commit. So, here I was cleansing a soul I had no business fixing. I jeopardized my happiness at the cost of them not feeling pain. I wanted to spare those layers they were going to shed, that disturbing pain of heartbreak. I wanted to be the hero this time; I was tired of being the victim. I wanted to feel purpose. I didn't for one moment wish ever to fade away from the puzzle I was putting together of my own. It was easier to love them than unpack the haunting pain I buried. I don't know why it was lighter to love the broken. Maybe it was a reflection of myself. Perhaps because I vowed to love myself, and I let myself down. Perhaps I was afraid to admit I was broken too.

I rejected self-love
I chose self-doubt,
self-sabotage
and self-pity
more times than I could count.
These thoughts were self-harm,
when I let myself be a fugitive to the abuse.
A danger to myself,
those dark thoughts I couldn't let up

-   *anxiety and depression aren't a good
    mix*

The love I planted in everyone else
I used to envy
until it didn't bloom.

I planted that same love
within me
and it thrived.

my garden consists of reassurance and
softness

-   *the key was always patience*

Temporary void

I was the codependent love,
the quick stop during the storm.

I was a home for the vacant
until they reached their next destination.
Until they abandoned me
when they started to heal.

I found comfort in lonely nights,
my temptation with pain,
rejection and adaptation.
I forced romance often.
In my defense,
I had no clue what love was
so, an ice box for a heart
felt like the best defense mechanism.
Sorrow was the melody of my soul

-   *and I was okay with it*

You will never find me where you left me,
I refuse to standstill
when growth is always an option.

Talking to myself ||||

I think it's so pure when someone finds me along their journey, chooses me, loves me, and grows with me. Even if it's not written in the clouds for a lifetime, the imprint I will carry gracefully, the pain too.

Who I love and who loves me,
will always be significant to my story.

No daddy issues

The kids at school would say, "your dad is so funny, he's so cool," and I believed it to be valid until your good at faking caught up to you. I remember everyone saying, "you look like your dad," which made it more complicated when you disappeared. I had to be remembered for someone I was trying to suppress. I guess you thought being without you would be best when you left without reason. You came back without an explanation. I had to live wondering. Do I continue this pattern of loving people who are good at faking? Who was good at leaving? Do I continue this cycle of trauma because I couldn't find the closure to accept it? I replayed this behavior when I ghosted people because I couldn't handle hurting them until I hurt them more by not letting them feel worthy enough. I wasn't worthy enough to be good to them, to love them the way they deserved, because I was a coward. Because I couldn't love myself enough. Those are the words I prayed to hear from you. Instead, "I don't know" was your reason. I thought not knowing was torture when I blamed myself for all the failed relationships. I chased people I let love me, and they always left me. It cost me years of suppressed trauma, broken situationships, and toxic traits. If I had to choose, I would not decide to know, overhearing you say

"I don't know"

It's like you were confirming that I was worthless.

Family is my sanctuary,
my safe place to go,
my shelter during the storms.
My sacred love,

-   *I'm not only talking about blood*

I'm not loyal by default.

- *It's a privilege to feel my love*

Jazz

I have never felt a love like the love you bring to me. I never thought I could love someone this much. When I see you, the way your eyes light up, and your little smile, warms my heart. You make me feel like the greatest soul. I will always protect you from this cold world because that's what aunties do. Watching you grow has been life-changing. I pray our bond never breaks, and you always see me as your best friend. I pray you always think of me when Miguel plays. I pray you always remember our music video sessions, dancing, and singing. I pray you always remember the inspiration and every blissful moment. You inspire me more than you know by giving me, unconditional love. To understand how easy it is for you to spread happiness and love, I pray you always keep that gift of softness. I pray you never let this world change you — a clever, courageous, and pure soul. You will always be my favorite.

Family moments

I don't know if I was naïve when I laughed at every drunken moment. My family threw a party just because it was Saturday. I grew blessed with a huge family, so it was bliss when we could come together. I was too young to drink so I would watch everyone sip and dance. I watched them slowly change into free spirits, open and full of life until it became night; one outspoken soul turned it to rage. Dysfunctional functions, I never understood why they became monsters. There was always tension. There were words thrown around, fists too. The worst thing my parents tried to do was try and hide it from me until it became more apparent as I grew. I found a way to see the true colors of some of my loved ones, some I live without til' this day. I stopped making excuses for them because they were "family" … I chose to see their true colors instead, all living red flags. They're ghosts to me now.

Addiction comes in all forms.
Drugs.
Abuse.
Sex.
Isolation.
The Internet.
Body dysmorphia.

An impulse to escape reality, to this place of comfort where they feel safer than their natural state of mind. Some feel secure in their dreams. Some never feel a source of calm energy because of the ghosts of their trauma, haunting and taunting them around every corner. The vice they choose frees them from the pain, even if it's just a moment. They search for healing in their thrill until they're alone and reminded by the demons; it's a revolving door to find relief in something that makes you weaker. Addiction can come in many forms, and not all are bad, not until they're intoxicating you into losing your treasure of a soul until you are lost and homesick at the thought of being without it. The constant chase isn't worth it.

Momma's Prayer

There's not much in life I'm fearless of, except losing the one who gave me life. My heart breaks just thinking of the day it happens. To be present many times, I needed to deal with the trauma of a loss. I watched my mother break when she watched her mother pass in front of her. I was young; I didn't even know how to comfort her; I was terrified to feel that same pain. I ran away from the thought of mourning. Grief was something more of a pushover. I see the broken heart she still lives with, which made me feel helpless. I pray she feels the bliss we bring to her, and the absence of her parents feels less, knowing they're still near. I pray she feels them still, and she knows they're proud of her. I pray that the trauma and pain find a way to break free. I pray she finds the key to set it free. I pray she never feels lonely. I pray she stays healthy. I pray she knows how much I love her, how much of a treasure she is, a strong woman, one who gave me life. I pray she never forgets how much she should be celebrated. I pray she never fails to love herself too.

Talks with the Moon

Sometimes I feel like I did things entirely wrong. Like if I would have let go of the illusion and realized that maybe there were some I wasn't meant to be in love with, or times I undressed the desire, hoping a stimulating moment would make them love me. There were many times I was ashamed of my actions. I don't believe I'm a saint at all; I just spent a lot of time setting fire to it, hoping it would burn away. Instead, it burned me. It followed me and preoccupied me until I took accountability. I danced around the idea of letting go too many times. I even made the excuse detachment would make me cold, so I suffered until they finally let me go. I was clumsy, clingy, and colliding when it came to love. I did anything for it; it was my drug of choice. I chased for a fix. I ended up withdrawing every time I was left in the dark and played, yet I went in this circle of lust until I opened my eyes. I was searching for love but accepting what was far from love.

Passive-aggressive,
my lack of control
my fear of rejection,
never condescending.
I was far from being in control
I lost myself often.

One of the hardest things to digest
was to understand I could love someone,
but I couldn't save, fix, or heal them. I could
only stand by them, inspire them, and
always do right by them.

A heart so heavy. A mind that's cluttered. Chaos crept up every corner. *Anxiety and depression* became my best friends. Except I tried my best to escape them, they lived rent-free. I thought they would kill me, but that's just another thing they tricked me into believing.

If I didn't have you,
I wouldn't have survived the storm of my
unhinged thoughts. The fears of my
unforgettable memories that I wished to
suppress. I wouldn't have been sane in the
ways I ended up. I got lost in my mind
when it hit 2 A.M., and my thoughts came
to intrude. My dreams disturbed me too.
The way I could take a feeling and recite it,
replay it, and digest every moment of it. It
surprised me. It took a massive weight off
me. In my darkest hours, you were there to
protect me. When depression created an
outlet for anxiety and all my other
insecurities to join, you were the refuge
from it all. I choose you every time. I
continue to choose you.

- *writing saved my life*

I'm someone who holds a connection close, who doesn't open up to just anyone. If you don't come with a beautiful soul and a passionate heart, I don't want you around me. I don't have what it takes anymore to keep letting tainted love ruin me.

I wasn't always someone who led with an open mind; I always led with a heavy heart. One I let burden me most of the time. I reacted off impulse of what my heart wanted. It never wanted to move on or hear anything timeless. I believed in it forever. I believe love could conquer all, and if it didn't surface with time, it would. I thought the timing was everything. Now I take the time I'm given and cherish the moment. I believed in second chances until I gave too many. I thought I could be loved the same way I was loved, but I always accepted every red flag that walked into my life without question. My heart cried for so long to fill this void of love so familiar but so out of reach. I just wanted to be loved, like soul deep.

To react or not,
a decision made often
when someone who didn't know me
would speak on me
so effortlessly.
Many times, I chose to correct them
until I learned,
I had nothing to prove
their inner demons
wasn't my responsibility.

Sometimes,

It's not even the cuddling; it's knowing
you're going to sleep next to the one you
love. There's so much comfort in that kind
of security.

Love note II

I prayed to feel this abundance of love you cater to me with. I prayed to have this kind of love reciprocated to me. I begged. I prayed. I had so much faith that I let everyone have a chance to prove they could love me. It was a risk I was willing to take. I can't say I regret always following my heart, especially since it led me to you. I don't regret the times I felt broken or the nights I spent crying because I've been let down again. I dealt with the consequences of all my biggest mistakes. Once I started cleansing my soul of those low-spirited, battered individuals, my life started to align. I fought so hard to keep replanting old seeds hoping they would regrow. I kept watering them until I was left dry. They never fully bloomed. But you, you were whole. You were a treasure to my heartsick soul. You brought a tenderness with you. I swore you were an angel. Your devotion was one I only imagined. I had to pinch myself often. I prayed it wasn't an illusion this time. I knew it was different this time; I didn't need to give you my heart as a keepsake for you to love me. You just loved me gracefully.

I made excuses for the narcissistic behavior.
The abuse in every form,
I was once codependent
to the dark, troubled
an infatuation so stimulating
it left me lovesick.

My dear melancholy,
you were fed
the wrong tale
of love.

Thank you to the ones who love me:

I owe a piece of my growth to you. You faithfully stood by me when I was drifting, searching, and witnessing myself. You helped me bandage the wounds. You opened my view to something more than the illusion I had in rotation. You were the warmth I needed to soften. You kept loving me even at my worst, even when I couldn't. I just wanted to tell you that your love is inspiring and has saved me many tears.

Seasons

We've entered fall: crisp air and beautiful leaves. Seasonal depression creeps; I'm terrified. The gloomy days are relaxing until it turns into weeks, then I'm lost like the drops of rain that make music when they hit my windows. Singing a song I find myself relating to, I'm often presented with darkness. Gloomy days can go either way. I thrive in the night when the moon's present, but I shine when the sun's out. My moods shift like the weather; I'm deeply connected. Mother nature protected me from the slump of depression this year. Please, let those dark thoughts fade; I can't handle another sad day.
I
Just
Can't
Do
It.
I want to have control every season.

Bubba

I hope doggie heaven
is treating you well.
My heart is still yearning.
I hope you found Poppy,
and that you are both reunited.
He was always his happiest with you.

I miss you both dearly

"**Regrets**": *a reflection*

I gave up on regrets long ago. I hold
everyone accountable for the pain they
brought me. Yes, I hold myself accountable
too. To regret is to have this power of
resentment that takes over, and every
mistake feels like a waste. To regret is to
wish things could be undone or redone
differently. Everything that happened
shaped me. I can't be ungrateful. I can't
expect it to happen differently when it's
already been done. I gave up thinking
everything was a waste of time when I
spent moments of my life with someone
who ended up not good for me. I grew from
the situation and came out a better me.
I spent years chasing a love that ended up
not for me, I learned what love wasn't, and
someone out there would give me the love I
desperately needed. But first, I needed to
provide that love for myself. I spent years
wishing to rewrite history to fix

disconnected connections, not realizing the direction wasn't for me to play God with. I had no control over what was written for me, but that didn't stop me from writing my own story. I loved some of the wrong souls, but they taught me so much about myself in the end. I let someone love me that didn't deserve to, they taught me to keep my heart open, but my soul closed; not everyone deserves that gift. I let some walk over me, tried to tell me who I was, and taught me not to chase love. To not pursue this idea of being loved and happy, these two emotions can't be given to me without filling my cup and setting the foundation. I was searching for someone to love and make me happy, that taught me only to provide myself with those things, and they could only add to it. I made countless mistakes. I chose the wrong ones many times. I was blind to what was for me and what wasn't. I let myself and my heart get destroyed over my definition of love. I allowed myself to become a different identity to make someone love me.

I lost myself entirely and found myself differently. Every regretful wasted moment and mistake has led me here. Who I am now is someone wise, beautiful, and at peace. Everything I needed, I found when I let go of the resentment of everyone who hurt me, and when I took accountability, I let them. I couldn't resent the journey, it's bittersweet, and it's exactly where I'm supposed to be. Why would I regret something that made me someone much more wonderful? I can't, and I won't. Every lesson was played perfectly, even though I didn't want to feel the pain, the sleepless nights, and the endless tears. What I wanted was nothing I needed.

Remember that before you choose to regret it. Remember how beautiful you are and who you're growing to be. It's always going to be a wild ride. So be patient and enjoy every moment.

Therapy

When I lost someone close to me, I sought out therapy. I wanted to make sense of the feelings and find a way to process them. Death is always hard to accept. We all know we're temporary, but it still hurts like hell. So, I decided to speak to a stranger for guidance. She tried searching for past trauma; sometimes, it felt like she wasn't listening to me. She was convinced I was hiding something, like being honest about why there wasn't good enough. I mean, she was correct; there was a lot under the surface. The trauma of my father disappearing and showing up ten years later. The trauma of being taken advantage of the first time I fell in love, giving myself to someone I loved, and bruised me. The trauma of losing many close to me. I was filled with trauma, but there was a specific reason I was there.

In her words, "you seem to have it all together" "Why are you here?". So, because I was good at articulating my emotions, I didn't need someone there. I felt alone. I had no direction. She gave me no guidance but wrong directions. I checked myself out and decided to stick with my notebook. I didn't feel it in me to keep reliving this story and all of me to multiple strangers just to find the one. I could only heal myself; I know that now. I know that therapy works for some, but it wasn't for me. I think that's okay. My talks with the moon ended my therapy. I found all my answers there. It's the safest place I have felt in a long time; I always find myself back there.

I know
what it's like to love someone
so much
and at the same time
be heartbroken, conflicted
because they didn't
love me too.

I'm a sucker for a compliment from a stranger. The bliss it brings, knowing they don't see the war I'm at with myself. Instead, they see my natural element. For a quick passing moment, it's enough to make me feel grounded.

The empath

I'm someone who tries to see the good in everyone, who extends myself to make sure everyone else is good.

Someone with a huge heart, sometimes it's bittersweet, to have this capacity of love to give when there's no guarantee it will be returned.

One night stand

I didn't think I was the type to spend just one night. I was an emotional being; I chased love often. Sometimes I spent the night for fun; sometimes, I thought love would evolve. I never gave myself to someone I didn't feel comfortable with. I don't think it makes me troubled to spend one night with someone I had a connection with. It was rare when it came to it. I had PTSD when it came to sex; I've been taken advantage of by someone I let entirely blind me. I trusted them. I loved them so much. I made excuses for the pain and faded those dangerous memories. I convinced myself they loved me and didn't mean to hurt me; even though "sorry" was a word played often, I listened and replayed it like it was my favorite tune. I suppressed the pain in this dark place, so I was terrified when it came to sex. For the first time felt like my purity got ripped away without a say. It was painful, and that feeling haunted me. I thought to myself often, "is this shameful pain going to revive every time" "is it always this painful" and "are they always going to take it without consent." I was nineteen when I lost my virginity. I wasn't thinking of sex; I was thinking of love and what I felt for them. The memories of that day are blurry and vivid; I remember saying stop, but they kept stroking. I cried as the pain wasn't leaving my body; I felt weak. They didn't take the time to map my body; they didn't care to unravel the beauty of the woman's body; they just wanted to feel good, even at the sacrifice of my pure soul. I was ashamed. I felt like a hostage to my own body. The tragedy I was left with from the memories. The bruises I hid so gracefully. I hid secrets so deep I felt humiliated by them. I couldn't free myself from them. So, I was never a "spur of the moment" kind of woman. I needed a connection. I needed someone fragile like me. I needed someone soft who unlocked that source of comfort. Even if it didn't end in love, a relationship, or we never crossed paths again. We know what we felt. We held no ill intentions after. Two souls who needed each other at that moment. A connection that was never meant to amount to anything but detachment. They gave me the gift of tenderness after the cure of being cold.

Moon hour thoughts

Death is so heavy,
my heart can't even ache,
my lungs can't even breathe,
my soul can't even be free.

I ponder, over and over
I just cry as I remember,
we're all striving to stay alive in this
temporary world.

Live in the moment, not forever.
Never pretend; love endlessly.

Please don't wait for your hometown to support you; they won't care until you make it. If you're passionate about your art, express it to the world. It may be terrifying, but people from all over the world are ready to appreciate what your city can't give you.

There's something about people from your city and how they refuse to see your success. They're too prideful and egotistic. They see you for who they bullied you into believing you were, not who you are.

Walking away isn't a sign of weakness; it's a sign of strength. It's a sign of saving yourself when you're drowning from the pain you didn't create. Toxicity is one hell of a drug, one we often overlook because of love.

Ghost

I will settle
for any version of you,
I just want to be close.

My prayer,

I give myself permission to let go of everything keeping ties to me, so I can make room for what's meant for me, to align with me. I give myself permission to allow them in without the extra guard. I give myself permission to love and be loved the way I deserve, not the love I conditioned myself to believe, or I settled to make work. I give myself permission to set boundaries when needed, even within relationships with those I love most. I give myself permission to take care of home first, of myself. I give myself permission to plant seeds in areas of my life, in relationships, and my dreams. I will water them. I will refill the cup every time it's needed. I give myself permission to grow, be happy, and go for everything I want. I give myself permission to be free.

I have parts of myself I wished would go away, like somehow, they would disappear, and I would be healed. Somehow the pain I felt would turn into happiness, and my broken heart would be repaired and treated with love.

It took me a while to understand, to evolve, doesn't happen overnight, but it also doesn't happen without work.

The question always was,

- *how far would I go to love myself?*

I never intentionally pushed someone away
because I was afraid they'd hurt me.
I was the fool who would try and convince
myself they loved me.

I know someone loved me . . .

When they didn't make me feel like I
needed to compromise my brokenness with
their wholeness, they accepted I was a work
in progress. I didn't need to change or alter
myself to be seen, heard, or understood. My
passions didn't intimidate them. Instead,
they clapped and celebrated me like I was
their dream. They felt me, and when they
couldn't, they gave me the space I needed to
breathe. They brought patience, peace, and
bliss. I know someone loved me when they
loved me in my love language, not theirs.

I should have said "no"
more often,
instead of escaping into the discomfort
in false "I do,"
"I will"
and hollow "yes"
for the sake of someone's pain.

- *they didn't deserve that kind of
  deception*

Misunderstood

I feared being misunderstood. I feared the feeling of not being good enough. I feared the thought of not fitting "in" or being accepted. I feared being the outcast, not the norm, and not having a voice. I worried myself into believing I needed to be accepted to be important. I stressed myself into believing being misunderstood meant I wasn't worthy.

Until I rejected this façade,
and accepted
there's so much beauty in being
misunderstood, like knowing

- *only some could feel me*

Jealousy is one hell
of a weakness
but has no home in me.
I hold no ill intentions,
I clap for others when they win.
I don't hold the energy
to give anyone questionable love

-   *I'm a real one*

Shame played its part in my life every time I opened my mouth without reflecting first. When I was hurt, it was my first defense to hurt them even worse. I spoke words that held no remorse. I feared rejection, so it was a shame that spoke when I picked up on ill intentions. I tried to stay silent. I tried changing my way of mourning. I made mistakes out of spite of the pain inflicted on me. I didn't collect regrets; I didn't feel it was right for me to be the only one hurting; after all, it was never my intention.

- *So, why do I feel ashamed?*

Apologies I'm owed:

I think I deserve a genuine apology from those who brought harm my way. I believe they must be aware of the pain that weighed a ton that I carried with me every day. If they could feel me, I wished to hear them say:

"**Hey, Sara**,

I'm the Capricorn you hate. <u>Your EX</u> that won't ever be forgiven. I can't use "I'm sorry" because those words often lost meaning when I played them out. I hurt you so severely; your forgiveness was like a revolving door; your second chances became unlimited. I became a monster when I let you hallucinate this façade. I let you believe I would do right by you when I didn't even have the intention of doing so. You were a pure soul that I saw so much potential to help me better myself. I used you for my gain. I used you to escape my reality because you were peaceful and the softest soul to ever get close to me. I loved you, but not for the reasons for you to love me too. When you said no, I should have listened. You were fragile, and I already played on your heart, so not listening to your consent, I don't deserve your forgiveness. I don't deserve to ever get access to you. I don't deserve to know who you are now. I just want you to know I'm accountable. I'm aware. I will live with hurting you; the ghost of your pure soul will never let me forget how much I regret turning the softest heart cold. You shouldn't live with that kind of burden; it's my punishment. I hope you found a way to be gentle again. I hope you found a way to feel secure after all I did to break you."

It's wishful thinking to hear those words. Words that held meaning, acknowledgment, and accountability. Instead, I received endless "I'm sorry" without an actual back story, but "I know I hurt you." that type of conviction deserves to be noticed and reflected. A simple "I'm sorry" doesn't amount to the trauma I dealt with years after unlearning those patterns of "love" I withdrew myself from. I always told myself, that I hold everyone accountable for everything they did to hurt me until they could come forth doing so.

Here's another:

"Hey, Sara,

It's your <u>FATHER</u>; I spent ten years away from you. We lived in the same town. I have had the same job since you were born. I occasionally saw your family members who worked with me, but I never reached out to you. I watched you grow, but I decided to walk out and never see some of your proudest moments and your lowest. I wasn't there for your high school graduation. I wasn't there for you through the death of your grandparents. I didn't call. I didn't even show up for the holidays. I didn't even see my own family. All I did was leave you on my health insurance to be taken care of; even then, your mom's insurance covered the rest. I spent ten years walking the same streets, going to the same stores, and taking the same buses, but we did not cross paths until years later. I was gone a whole decade. I missed you, and I thought of you often. I couldn't be the father you needed me to be. I don't believe I had it together. I worked so much that I didn't have time. I never had my place; I always had roommates. I was ashamed of who you would see because I didn't even know who I was. I was hurt because your mother had someone else in her life; I took that as my cue to go. You would be better off. I fought your mother on child support; she had to get it through my paycheck. When you were young, one of my girlfriends convinced me, that you weren't my daughter even though you look exactly like me. I let people get in my head and decide what kind of father I would be. I should have stayed around and been there for you. It's my fault you lived to fill a void of love that was never reciprocated to you. It's my fault you spent years of your life having dysfunctional connections because you didn't trust people when they said they would stay. You started your path of ghosting because of me, running and suppressing the pain so you wouldn't need to feel it and keep reliving it. I should have told you it had nothing to do with you. I should have told you the exact reason instead of ghosting you. I still don't know why you gave me another chance; I know I don't deserve it. But I'm aware of my wrongs. I'm accountable."

My reflection: All I received was "I don't know" when I asked where he's been for ten years — a run-around of the truth. I decided to keep the relationship in my life, but to hold regrets was too heavy for me; I kept a guard. One I won't let shatter because he'll never be that close.

Here's another:

"Hey, Sara,

It's me, your <u>EX</u>, the one that was both comfort and hardship" I blamed you for a lot of what went down when our ending became a disaster. I blamed you for leaving me when it was also my fault; I put this perception into perspective when I manipulated you, gaslighted you, and made you my possession. I controlled what you posted on social media. I controlled what you wore. I got into your head and made it all about me. I found a way to make you feel your lowest and played on it. I always thought you looked better with makeup, so I encouraged you to wear it constantly. I also told another woman you looked better "in pictures" than you did in person, to get nude pictures of her or sleep with her. I wanted attention. You gave me a lot of attention, but honestly, I was troubled and devoted to the toxic. I wanted you, but I wanted other women too. Threesomes were most of our relationship because I played on your love for women. It was part of the reason we broke. I went to one of your family functions, the rest I was a ghost, but we were together for three years. You ended up around me more than your family, and you loved them so much. I was codependent and needed you near because of my lonely ways and traumatic past. My trust issues had me in a chokehold. I placed my insecurities onto you many times. I tap-danced around the idea of rekindling that toxic connection with my ex; I flirted with the idea; it had you questioning us. I supported you until I felt threatened by your success. I grew to love you, but more so, the comfort you brought with you. I should have told you I wasn't ready to love you the ways you deserved because I didn't even love myself the ways I needed. You were my void. I didn't intend the agonizing pain that became of us. It was irresponsible for me not to be accountable, to be conscious of the reckoning I brought to our relationship. I get that now."

My reflection: I was aware I did things that weren't the way I wanted them or the timing. In my defense, it was calculated in my head beforehand. It took me a while before I was able to see clearly. That meant my share of mistakes and pain I brought too. I took accountability for what I brought that burdened you; it's just, that I felt you used my faults to distract yours like you did everything else. We weren't meant to be any longer; I was acceptive of our ending. You, on the other hand, blamed me for everything. I just wanted you to acknowledge those things that bruised me, but you were emotionless unless it came to you. You were so selfish; why would I think you ever loved me?

I wish I didn't need to go,
but you are a mirror
of my deception,
I can't love you the same

-   *It's time to part ways*

I believe I was placed into this world to bring love, light, and healing. I think my words and experiences shed inspiration on those who need a friend, one that speaks and doesn't judge. Perhaps I'm someone who makes them feel less lonely, knowing they can relate to someone. It's like they're silently confiding in me. I believe in purpose, and I think I'm fulfilling mine. We're all searching for meaning and this sense of purpose; sometimes, it's already unraveling before your eyes. I have a special connection with souls I probably won't ever meet, but we have the same feeling while reading my heart on paper. That's special.

Think about what you love to do; imagine doing it, succeeding at it, and loving it. Your purpose will never disappoint you. Your purpose is whatever makes you feel safe in this cold world, something that won't make you feel alone.

10 things that *make me happy.*

1. My family

2. My fiancé

3. Music

4. The Moon

5. Beach days and summer nights

6. This is Us

7. Free Willy 1 & 2

8. Breathing

9. The relationship I have with myself

10. The happiness of others

It's a *hostile-filled world,*
I'm just here
trying to **stay pure** in it.

Someone who manipulates,
an impulsive deceiver.
A charming, alluring
and relief to be around
but who will starve you,
from the warmth you possess.
A con artist,
a hallucination at best

- *traits I never wished to adapt*

I envied those who were free,
So, I manifested it for myself.
I just wanted an ounce of confidence,
my shy soul begged for it.
My anxiety stayed on the clock.
Reserved. Introverted.

-   *why did I care so much?*

I found so much peace
in solace,
when I stopped attaching loneliness
to being alone
and found bliss
in my solitude.

- *I finally loved being my own*

10 songs that put me in a better mood:

1. <u>Anytime</u> – *Ray J*

2. <u>Care</u> – *Sonder*

3. <u>When Your Mad</u> – *Ne-Yo*

4. <u>Pineapple Skies</u> – *Miguel*

5. <u>Morning After</u> – *DVSN*

6. <u>Outlandish</u> – *DVSN*

7. <u>Blood flows</u> – *SOHN*

8. <u>Gave Your Love Away</u> – *Majid Jordan*

9. <u>Somebody Else</u> – *The 1975*

10. <u>Golf on TV</u> – *Lennon Stella*

June 27, 2021

12:05 p.m.

Twenty-eight, wow. These last four years of my life have been the most important lessons of my journey. I lost and gained so much. I grew and evolved into this soul I'm proud of. A soul I can identify. A soul I can say I love. I've conquered some of my biggest fears and chosen the unknown more times than I decided what gave me comfort. I parted ways with what I outgrew and everything that withdrew itself from me. I aligned with everything for me. I made an oath to myself at twenty-five, to never stay in an environment that isn't healthy; to let go and embrace only what chooses me. I kept promises to myself. My short-term and some long-term goals have been attained. I'm happy. I'm healthy. I'm surrounded by souls who love and bring a rare connection. I'm always struggling to love myself. I've been my own worst enemy throughout my journey; it's not easy. It's unlearning and trying hard not to repeat patterns and behaviors from old triggers or the insecurities I have coming to visit me. I have a better vision of myself today. I have a different connection with myself today.

Each year I'm proud of the woman I have become — a bestselling author. I'm engaged to an amazing man. My niece entered the world. I'm a full-time author. I'm blessed to spend every moment with the ones I love. To have beautiful people supporting me. I don't take any part of life for granted. I see life as a roller coaster, the fear of doing it and facing what comes next but enjoying the ride for however long and wherever it will take me. I'm grateful. I'm fulfilled.

Every year,
I will only
become more significant, wiser, and proud.
I love it here.

My skin was the broken side of me. The constant fight to hide the insecurity I tried so desperately to mask. No makeup could redo what I was dealt. I created this illusion I wasn't beautiful. My skin treated me like a burden because I was turned down for my breakouts. I thought to be transparent, to give myself to someone who would look past my flaws. It broke me. How was I supposed to love myself if someone couldn't love me?

I crashed. I closed myself off. There was nothing left inside me. What hope did I have left? Everyone I let close left.

At that time, it didn't make sense
For it to be them that didn't deserve me.

Love wasn't enough to keep someone
who wasn't meant for me.
To never dim myself down.
If I couldn't be my vulnerable self,
I couldn't be with them.
Their insecurities and trauma
Aren't mine to fix.

-    *saving someone isn't love*

I consider everyone who made me feel
something rare,
raw and real,
a soulmate.
even if they're no longer present in my life
their memory
and lessons
will forever be near.
I cherish it all.

Being in love with someone
who doesn't love you back,
Is like,
chasing a hallucination
and confusing it with reality.

I held a lot of people accountable
for hurting me,
that I put into play.
I asked some to trust me,
I vowed the layers they shed in front of me
would be safe

-   *my very first deception*

Some find it draining,
to cater to my consistency
of needing to be reminded,
constantly.

-    *a little reassurance never hurt anybody*

We were only meant to collide,
to destroy each other

-     *a canvas perfected in pain*

I'll never be a perfectionist
Nor do I want any in my life.
I'm imperfect in the ways I like.
I like knowing
I don't know everything.
I like learning new things.
I like being humbled.
Being perfect
comes with this mindset
of doing no wrong,
and I've done plenty

- *I'm not a liar*

Note to self:

I'm intensely passionate; I won't ever
apologize for that.

Remember,

Setting the wrong expectations of love and
the people you love isn't pretty, but love
will always be beautiful.

Grief is so heavy,
It's something that you carry forever,
In the shadows.
In the light.
It's something embedded in you.
You won't forget it.
It will always linger,
You find a way to survive with it.

I shrunk myself
to make some comfortable.
I held back my pain
to help heal others.
I was the stronger one,
the one who always needed to let go.
I protected everyone
while destroying myself

-   *the life of an empath*

There's no real love
In someone
who breaks your heart,
over and over
and watches you pick up the pieces.

Having a partner who supports you will help you reach your full potential and knock out the fear of never feeling good enough. It's essential to be with someone who celebrates you, inspires you, and never makes your dreams feel like they're not attainable.

This chapter is called
Peace,

I'm loving it here

Thank you for taking the time to read to feel me. It's always a pleasure spilling these emotions; sometimes, it hurts but freeing. I'm so blessed to have a platform to share my truth and help those afraid to share theirs feel less alone. I'm here.

I'll always be your friend.

My **platforms**:

Instagram: Moonsoulchild
Twitter: Bymoonsoulchild
Tiktok: Bymoonsoulchild
Facebook: Moonsoulchild
Apple Music & Spotify: Moonsoulchild

Moonsoulchild.com

All my **books**:

The Journey Through My Heart
Vol. 1 and 2

I Was Never Broken
Vol. 1 and 2

Letters To You

Dear Anonymous

YoungNakedSoul

Heal Inspire Love
Self-Talks
(co-write with Michael Tavon)

Soul of Cancers

The Feels the Moon & My Soul

The Feels the Moon & My Soul
(*Deluxe prompt version*)

The *Feelings and Healing* Collection:

Finding self
Healthy Connections
Grief

Discovering
Twin Souls
Broken

Soulmates
Healing
Insecurities
Toxic Connections

Printed in Great Britain
by Amazon